Copyright 2013

Ron Koppelberger

Surreal Secret

Website
Wolffray.blogspot.com
Farthermostdream.blogspot.com

Dedicated to YOU!!!!!!!!!!!!

Welcome

I created this scrapbook of art to entertain the art enthusiast in you. These are in the shape of surreal dreams and thoughts. If you spend a few moments looking at them they will reveal themselves to you in the form of stories and sometimes hidden revelation. This is art that is meant to be looked at more than once……..Enjoy!!!

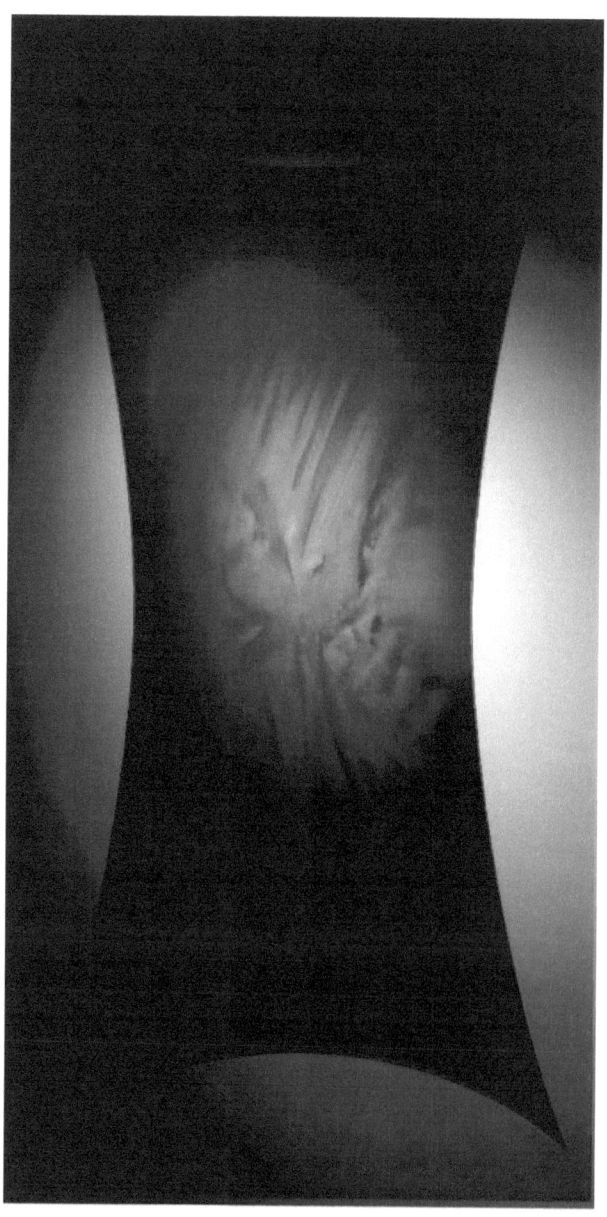

Lady Peacock In Black

Angels In Red

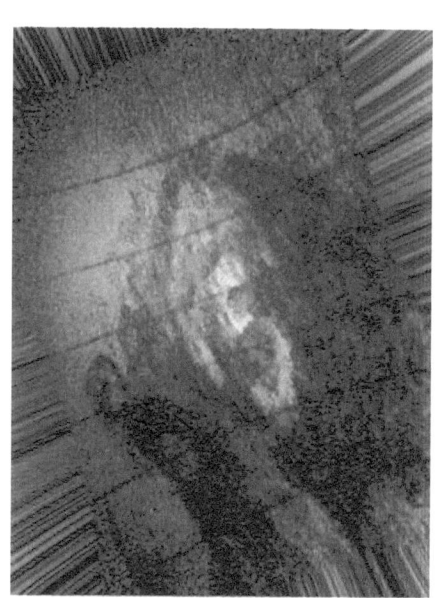

Woman In Misery and Contemplation

In Thought Crumbles

The Tears Of A Butterfly In Sorrow

Escape To Avalon

The Egg Hatching

My World In Focus

Woe In White

Her Flourish In Shadowy Light

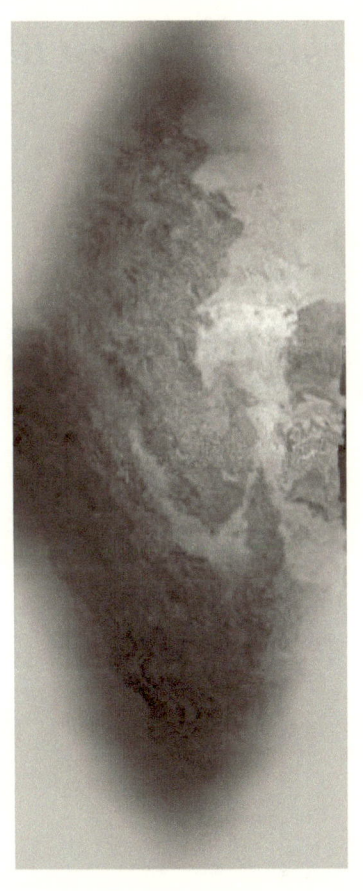

Praying In Earnest Blues

Images of a Dream In Tears

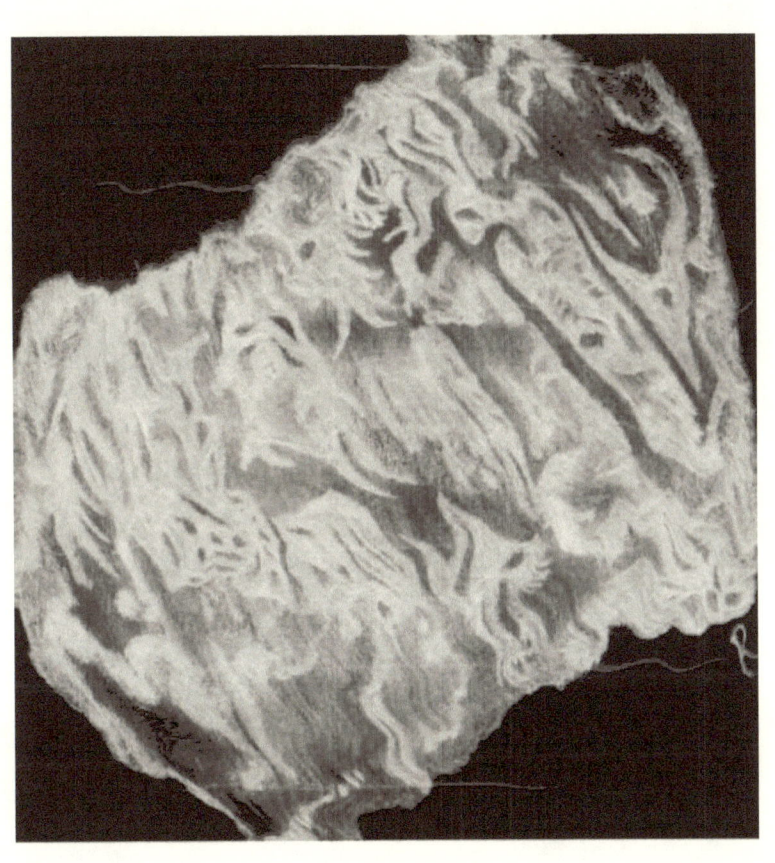

Everything In all And More

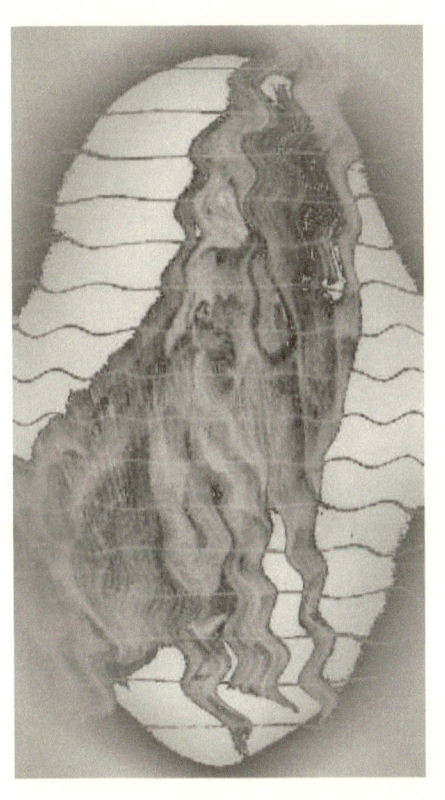

Dreamy Illusions

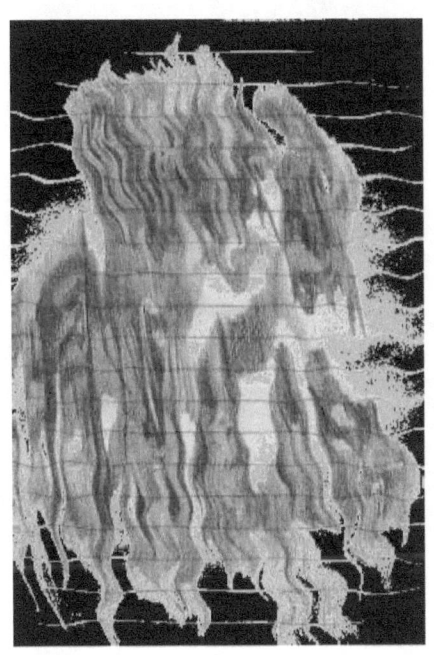

Nightmare In Motion

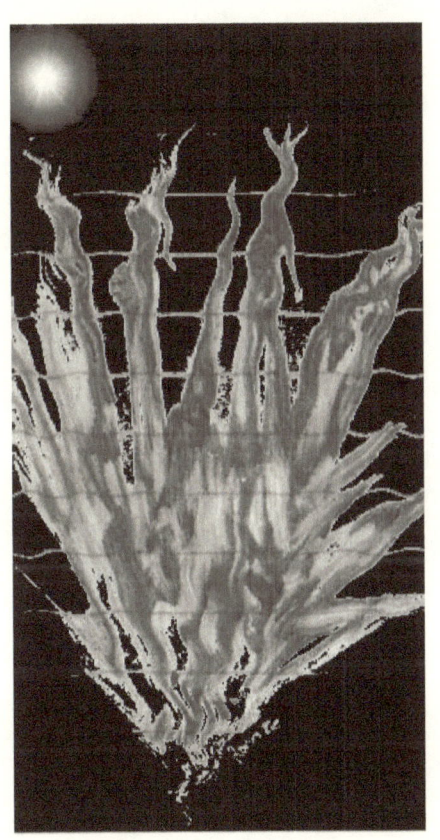

Weed In Cool Flame

Peering Through The Flames of Perdition

Faces and Shapes

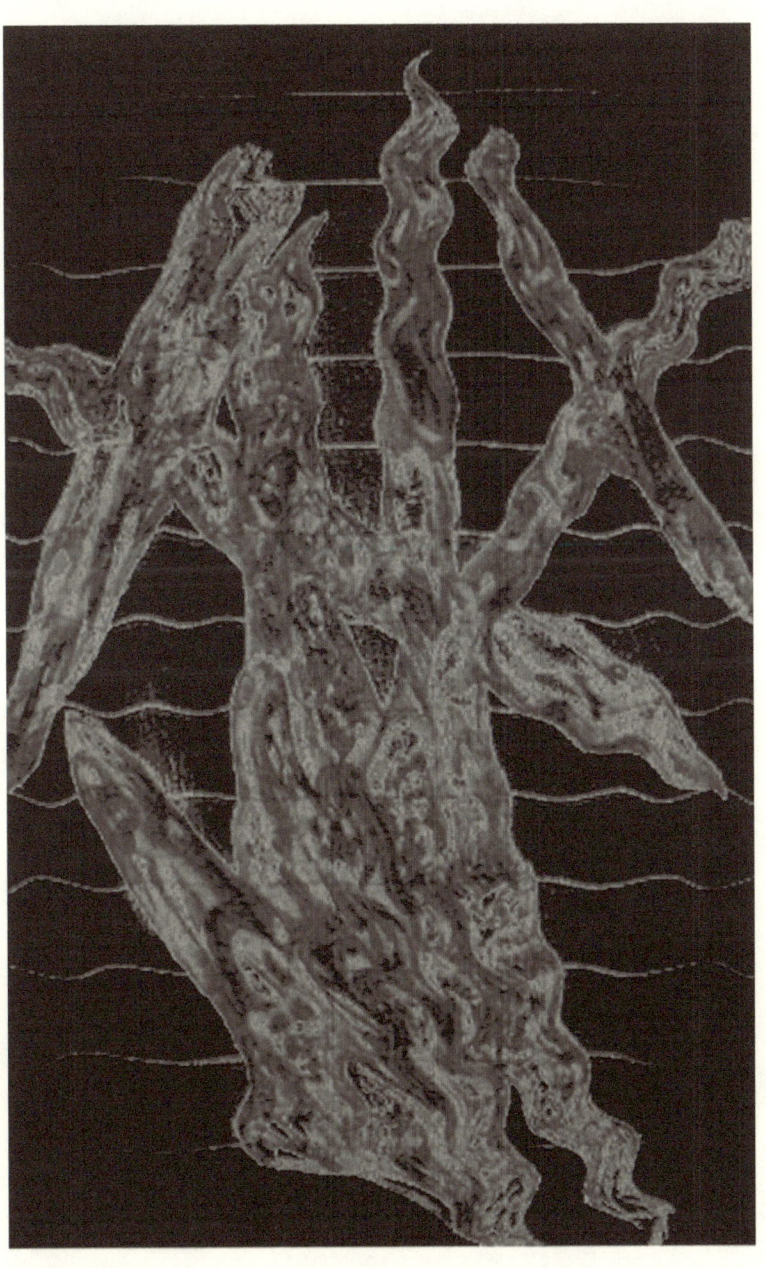

The Stork and Cross

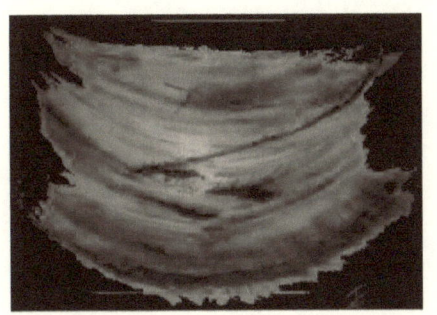

Madman On Fire

Lost In Thought And Dreams

Baby Blue

Angry In Perdition

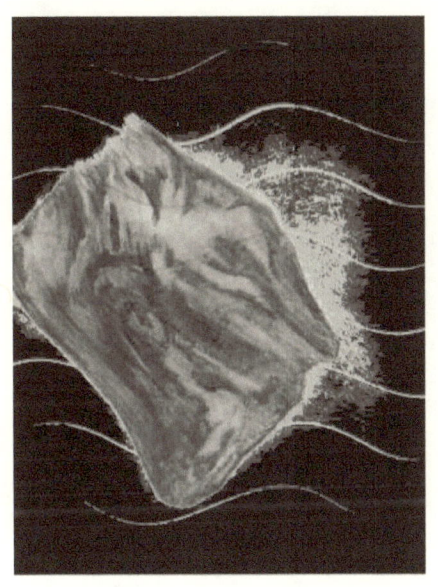

Ghosts In Her House

Dragon In Flame

Images In My Mind and Light

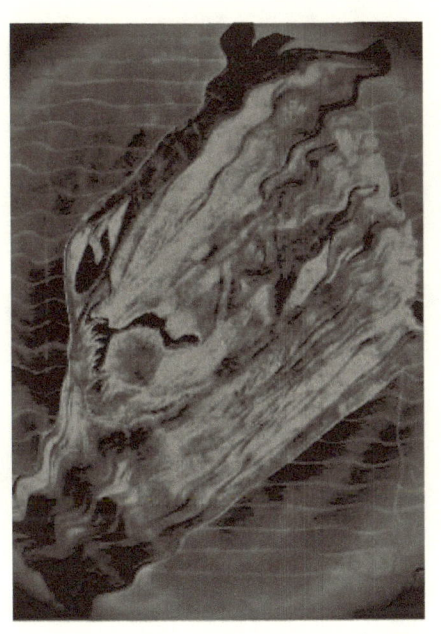

In Repose Within

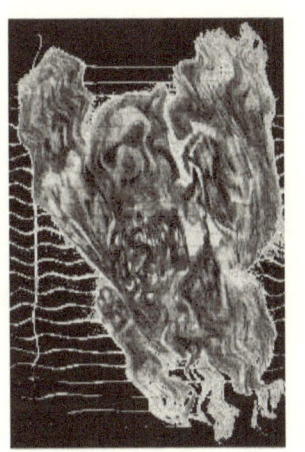

Bear In The Air

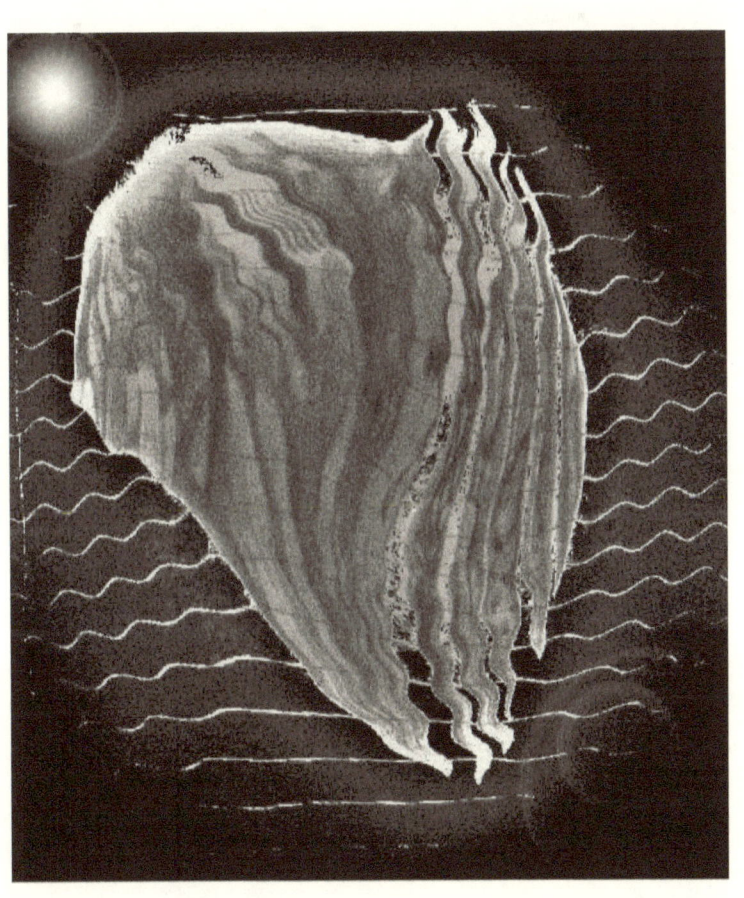

Slices Of The Sun

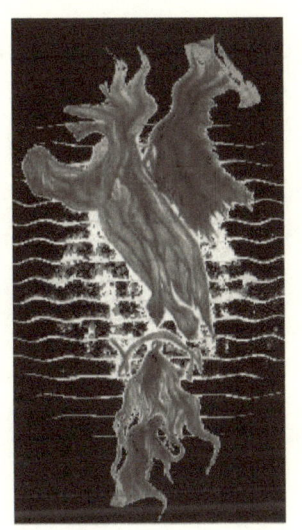

She Hides In Shadow

Horror In Crypts

Butterfly In Gray

Monster and Motion

The Bird In Contrast

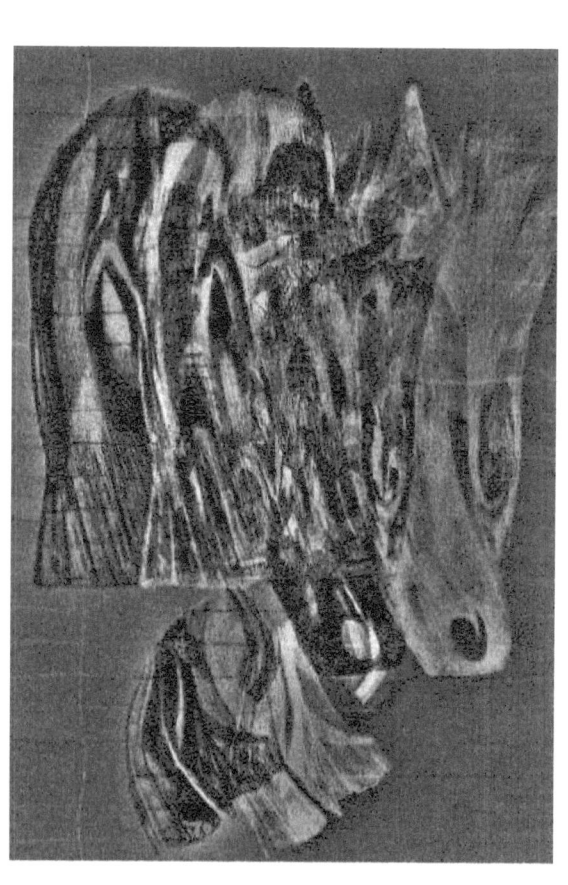

The Thumb and Doorway

The Alien In Colors

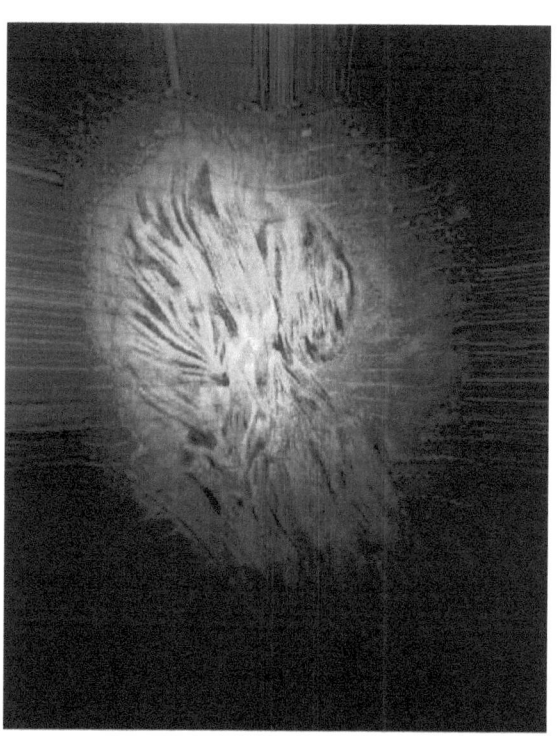

Caught By A Tiger In A Rush

Angels Unfolding On Him

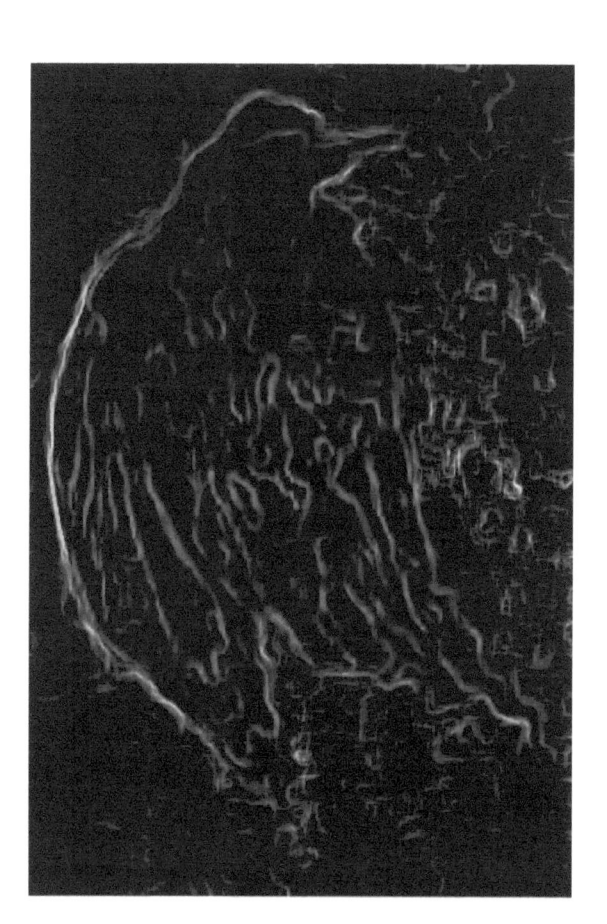

The Cloak

Native Feather In Blue And Red

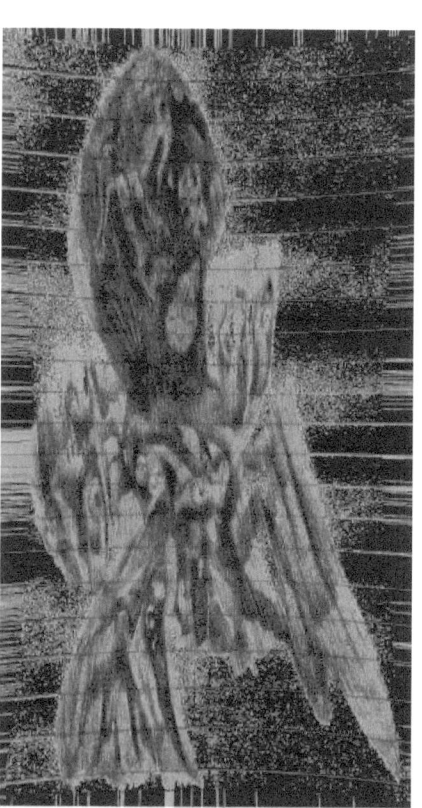

The Spider In Gauze

Halloween In Lights

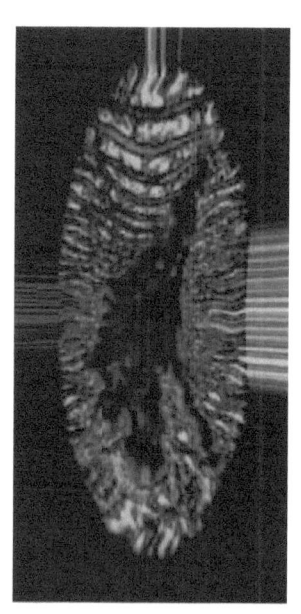

War Bonnet

Kerchief and Scream

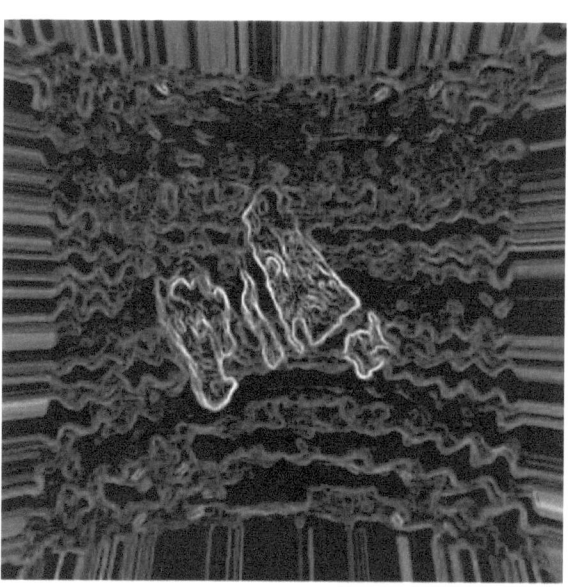

The Tiger and the Inca

Colorful Leaf

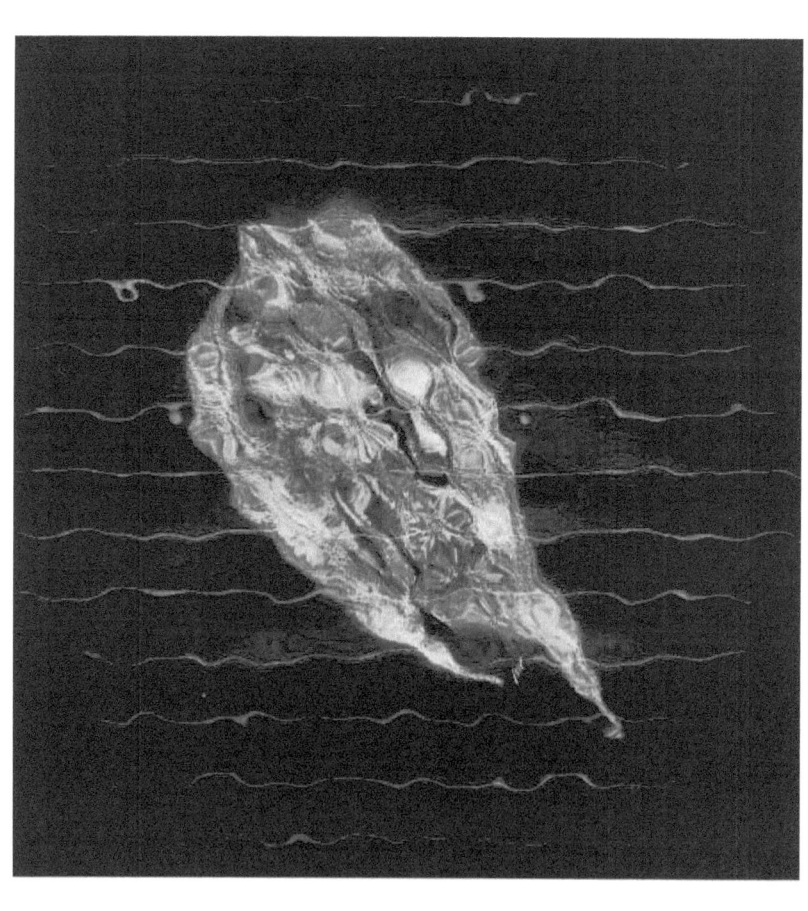

Bewildered

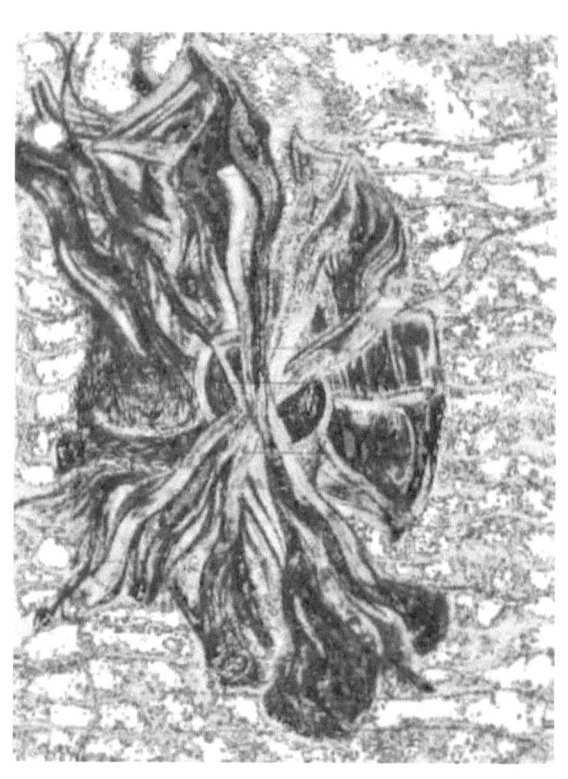

The Puzzle Picture In Flux

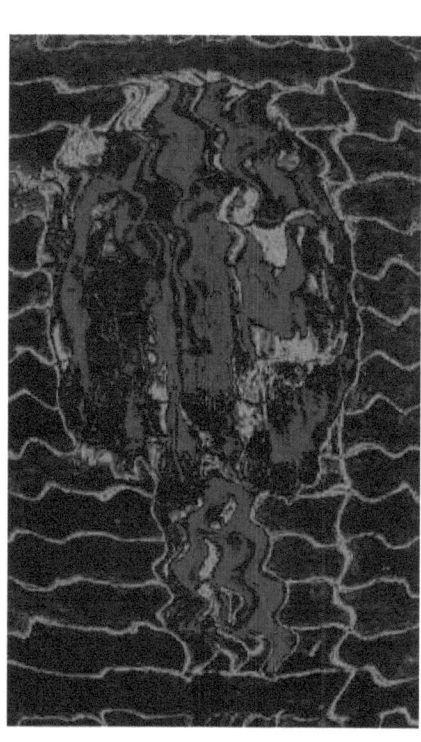

The Gnome And The Tree

My World In Shades Of Blue

Her Visions

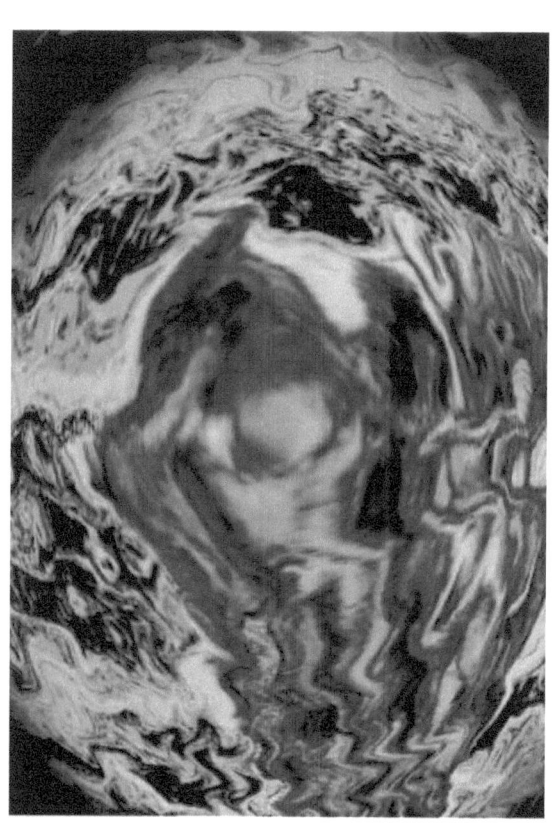

Looking From A Tempest

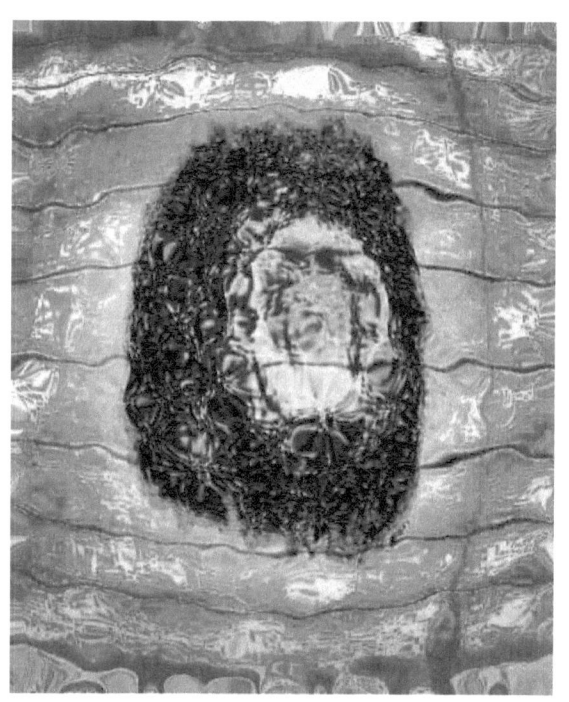

Looking Out

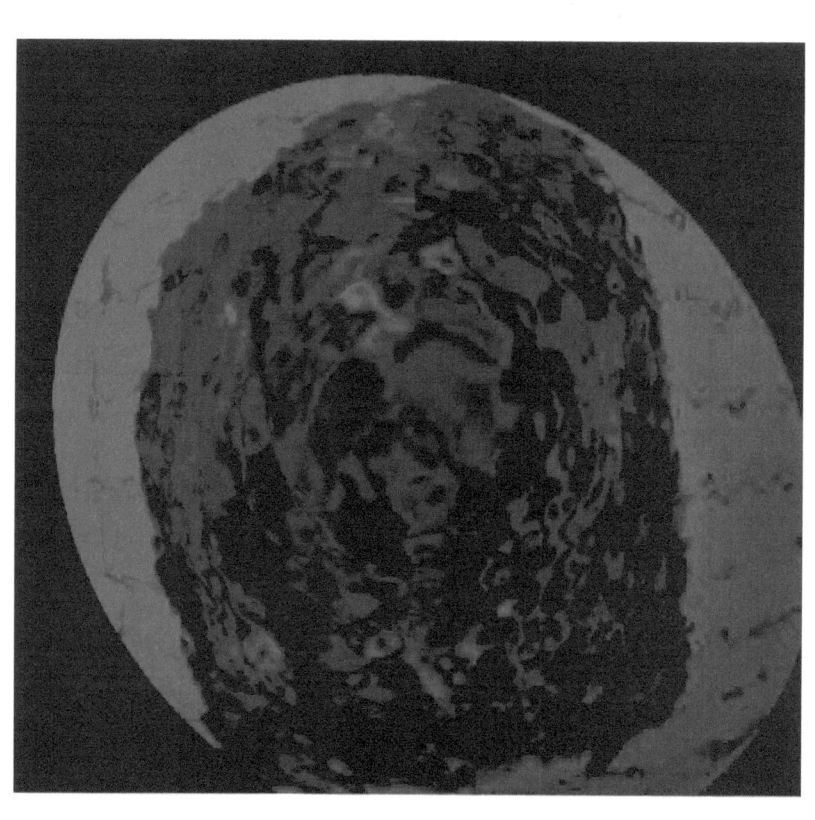

Caught In a Tempest

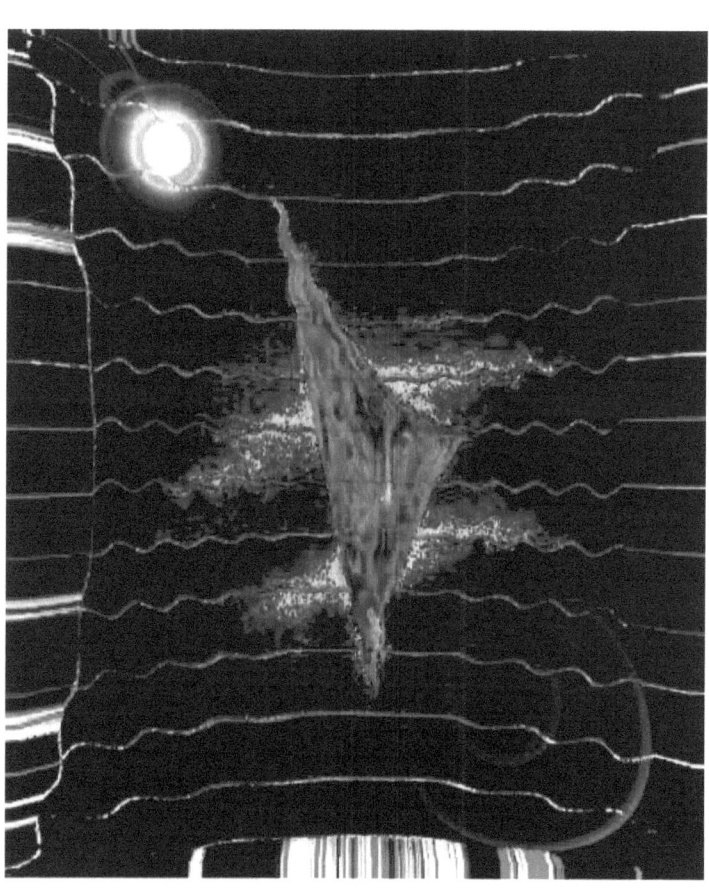

Bones And The Devil

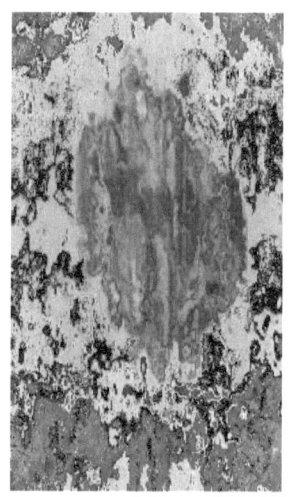

Lost Child

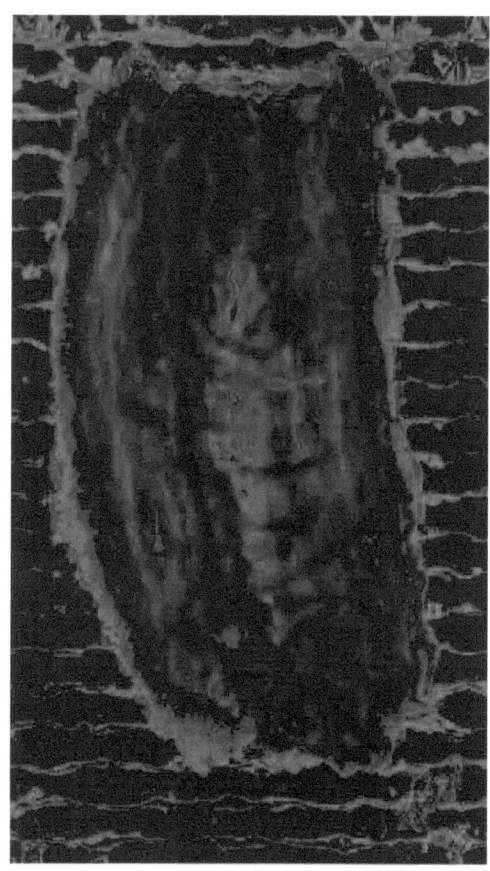

Coffin Sleep In Red

Ghostly Gray

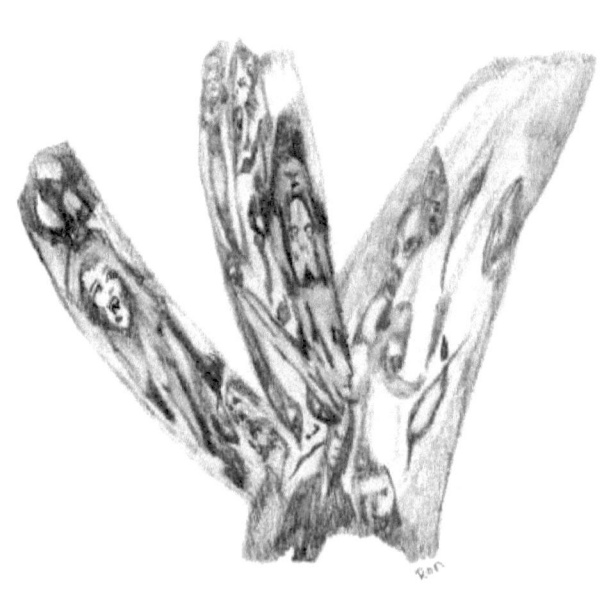

Three Paths

The Woods Around Me

Forward and Backward

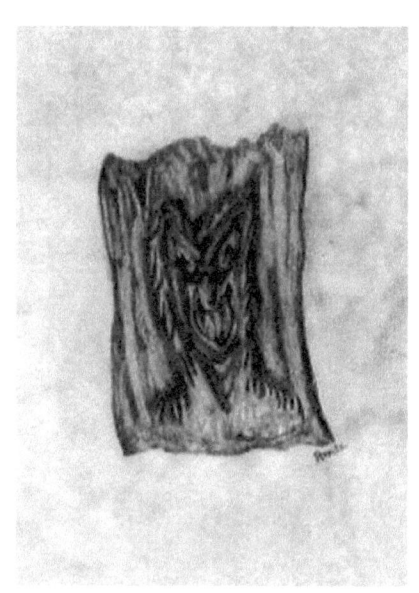

A Devil

Morphing

She Finds The Night

The Queen Of Shadows

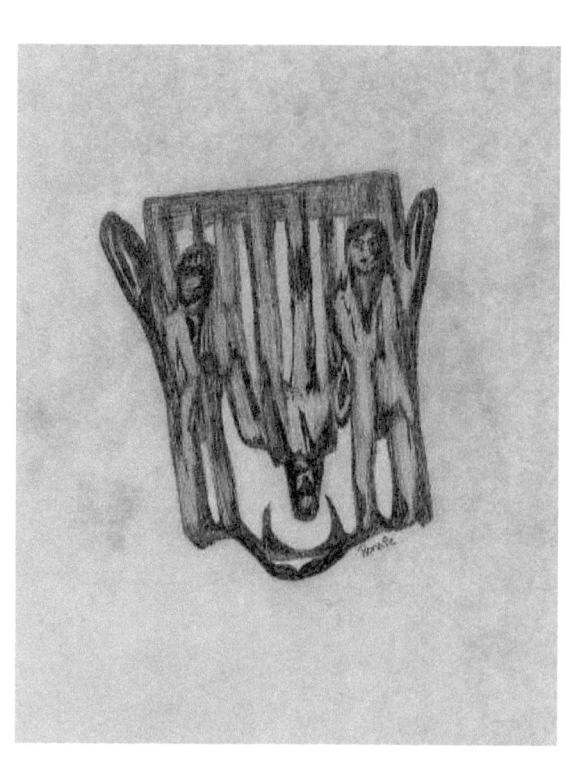

The Three

She Screams

Finding The Way

The Stump In Secret

The Monk

Jumbled Images of Fate

Four Globes

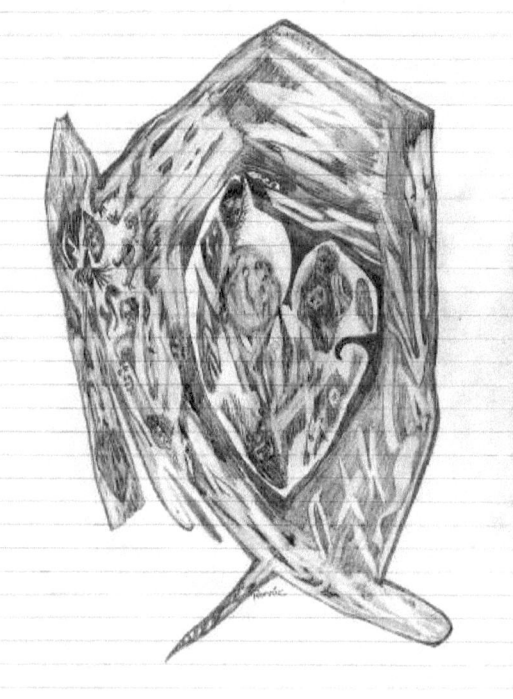

Full Circle

Facing The Door

The Bird

Ghosts

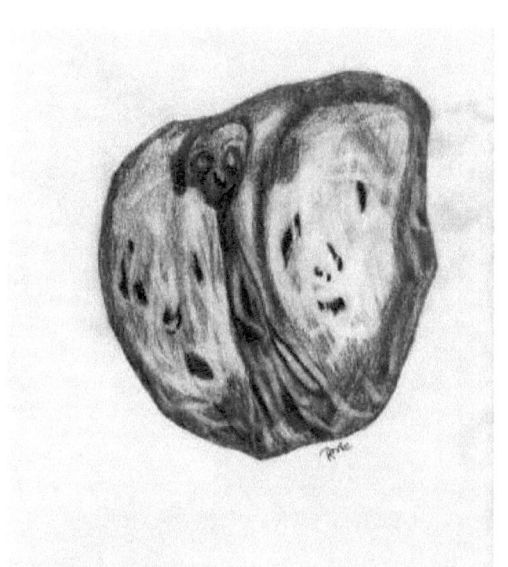

Jus Passin Through

Segmented

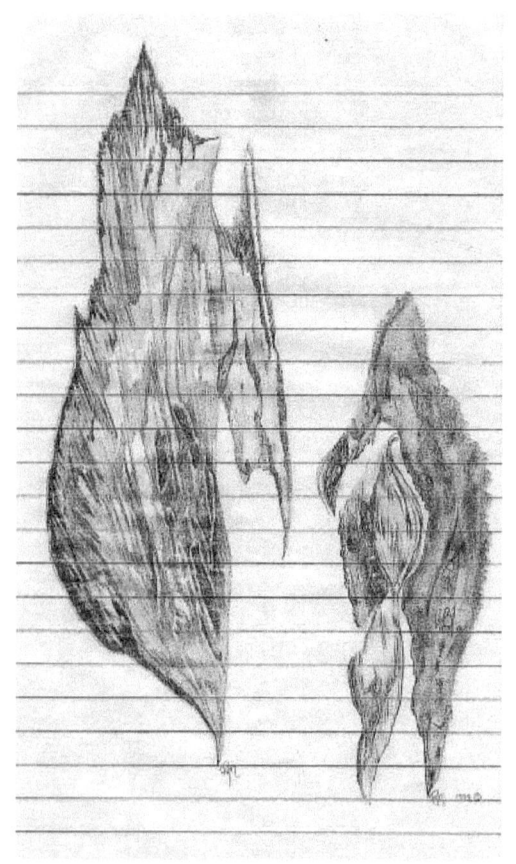

Asking the Sage

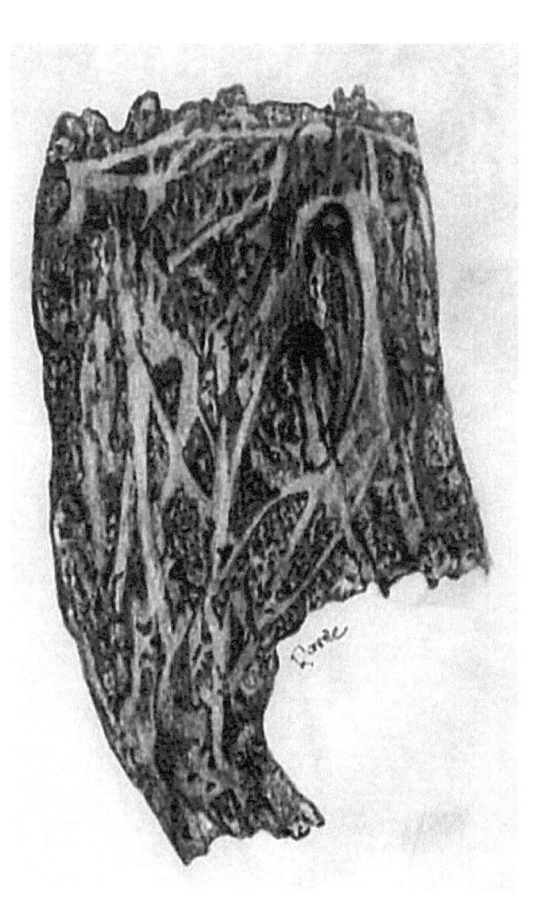

Metamorphosis

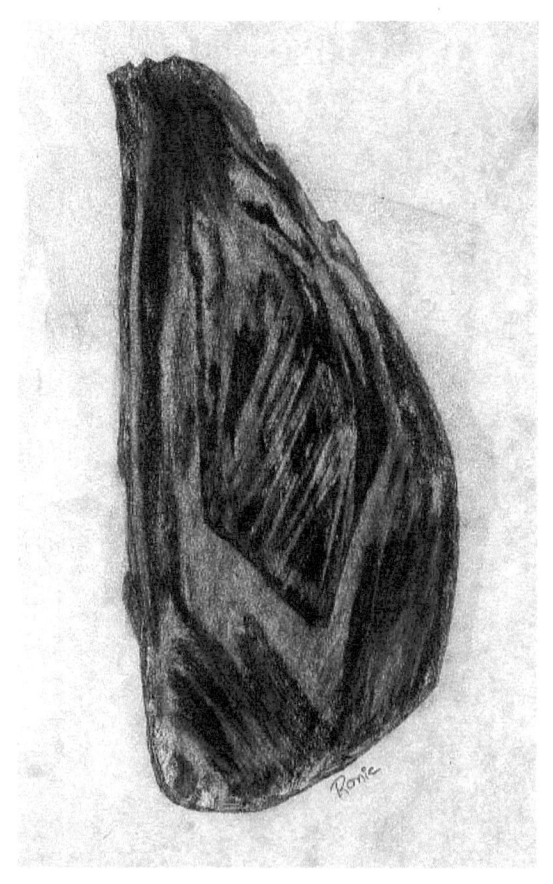

The Mummy

Hidden Wonder

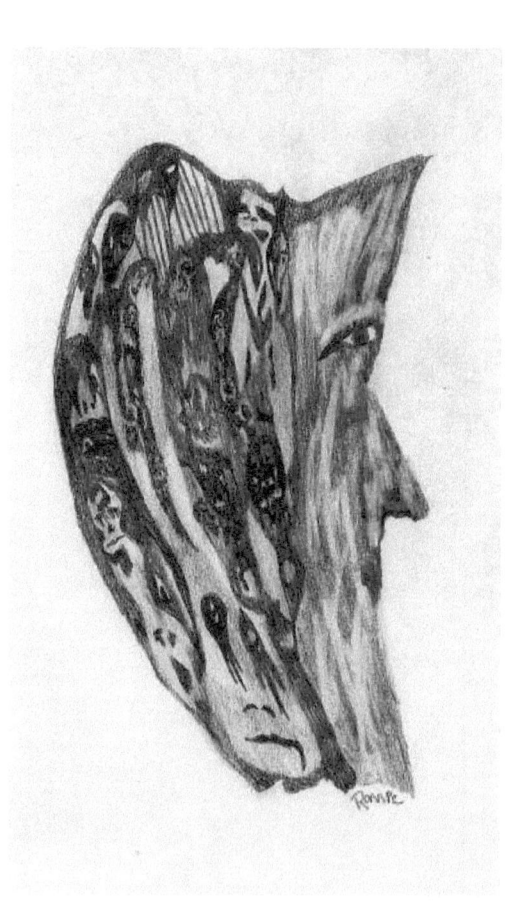

In His Head

Clouds of Color

Reflections In Blue

The One Who Watched

Porky Gets Scared

Looking Glass

Full Speed

On The Wings Of A Dragon

An Angel

Native Feather

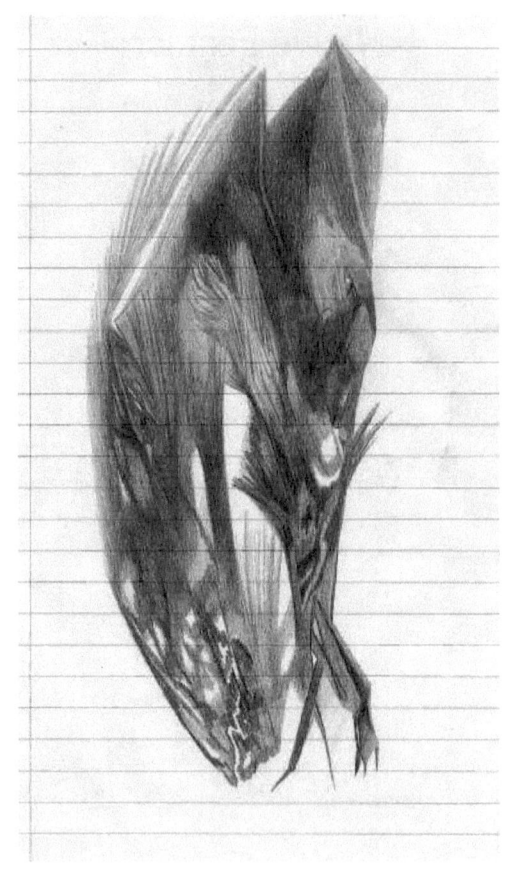

Witch Doctor

The Puzzle Picture

Alien Three

The Cat

The Knife Cut

Feathered Dragon

Hidden In Darkness

Comedy Vs. Tragedy

Extra Terrestrial

Queen Of The Butterflies

Lost Images of a Family

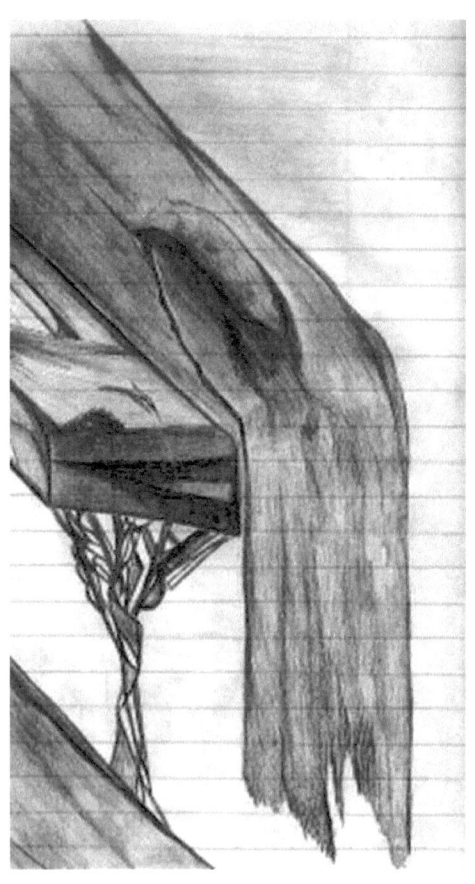

Wood Melting

Hung

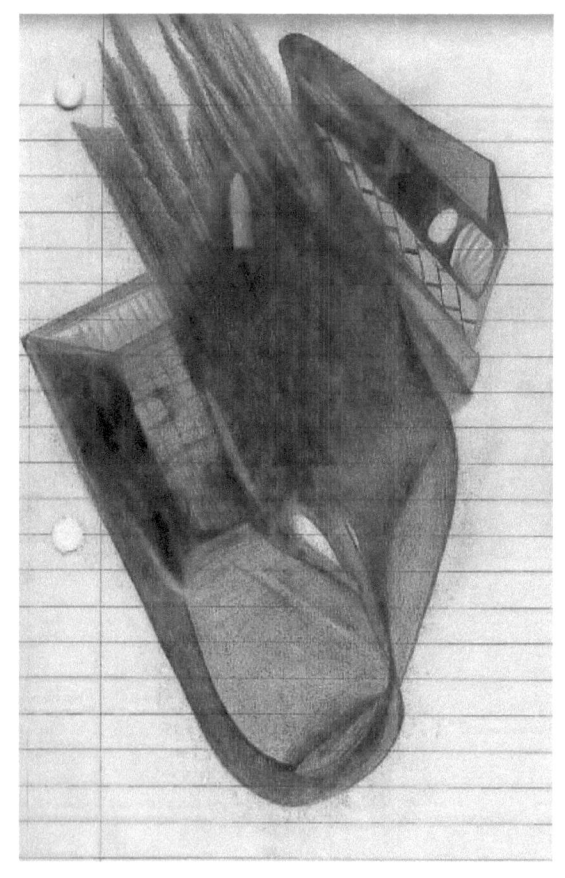

Oppression

The Shaman

A lien Encounters

The Swamp

A Crow

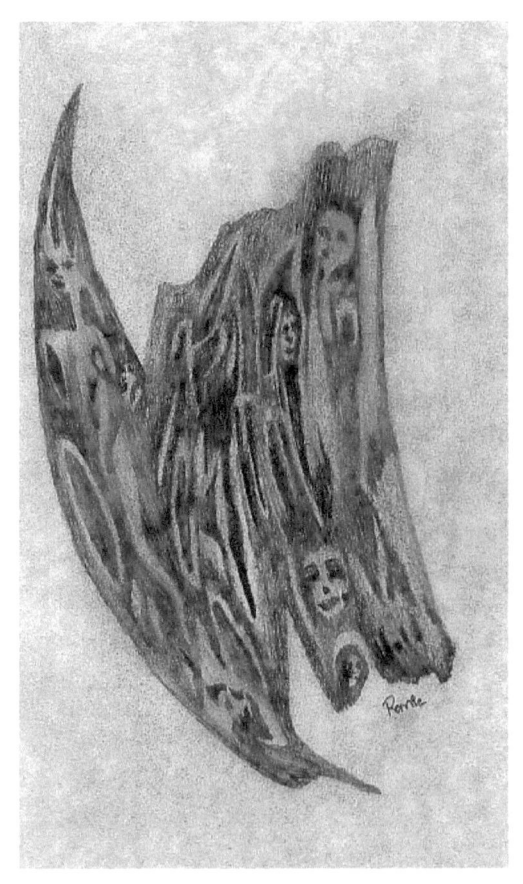

Hallow Looks

Looking Out

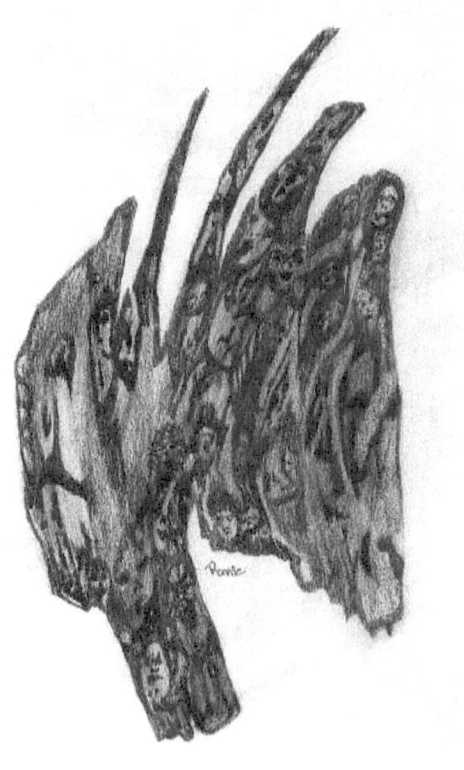

Butterfly Dreams

The Moth

Zombie Dreams

Thank You

www.ingramcontent.com/pod-product-compliance
Lightning Source LLC
Chambersburg PA
CBHW031837170526
45157CB00001B/332